The King's Hostage

The Story of Saint Margaret of Hungary

by

E. Virginia Newell

Illustrated by Pauline Eppink

A Grail Publication

St. Meinrad, Indiana

Nihil Obstat:

   Joseph G. Kempf, Ph.D.
   Censor librorum

Imprimatur:

   ✠ Paul C. Schulte, D.D.
      Archbishop of Indianapolis

January 22, 1948

Dedicated

To Margaret, Princess of Hungary, and to the beloved Margaret Slachta, Sister of Social Service and first woman member of the Hungarian Parliament, in whose life one can see the pattern of the Princess and the mothering of a nation.

Foreword

Standing below Budapest on a wooded island now famous in the kingdom of Hungary as a resort are the cloistered ruins of St. Margaret's priory . . . . The Convent of the Blessed Virgin.

Here, in the thirteenth century, Princess Margaret Arpad, daughter of King Bela the Fourth, offered herself to God's holy service in fulfillment of her father's promise.

Repeated invasions have destroyed all but the outer walls of the Priory and even the burial place of this gentle princess, but those who give their lives for eternal values cannot be forgotten. So it is that not only in the vine-covered ruins of her cloister on Margaret Island does the princess live again, but also in the hearts of all who can see beauty in fidelity, even when it is hidden away.

Chapters

CHAPTER I

The Promise

BELA Fourth, king of Hungary, the Land of the Magyars, and his queen, Maria Lascaris, stood on the island of Trau. From here they could see to the plain on the opposite bank, where the flat sandy lands stretched into a gentle slope. Along the shore smoke rose from scattered tents. Men scurried about sharpening weapons and lashing and unlashing their flatbottomed boats.

Bela turned to the queen, his face pale with fright. He had but a handful of men to support him. Most of his soldiers had met death, battling the invading Tartars now encamped on the opposite plain. Whole families of nobles had been wiped out and their castles and land burned and pillaged, while the faithful few remaining often strove among themselves for power.

The queen sighed as she looked at the white face of her husband. Bela was not a coward. This she knew, but now all seemed against him.

"Is there nothing I can do?" she asked herself, turning again to look at the opposite shore.

The men were loading picks and axes and long spears into their boats. Their dark faces were filled with fury as they hurried about, and the black braids of hair which hung down the sides of their faces shook with the energy of their movements. Watching this wild foe pulling and hauling their gear, the queen gathered courage.

"My dear husband," she began, "God has taken two of our children from us during three years of invasion and war. Now He is going to send us another child. Let us vow to Him and His service and the service of our country this child, if He will spare our people and our lands. If the child is a girl, her name shall be Margaret."

For a moment the king was silent. When he spoke, he reached his mailed arm toward the queen and, kneeling, drew her down beside him.

"Our child to be an offering if God will spare our people and our land," he said. "Who but you, Maria Lascaris, would be so generous? So be it."

Again and again the king and queen repeated together the words of their promise as above them dark clouds pushed their way across the sky until they were directly over the small island of Trau. Here they broke, spilling themselves in a torrent of rain. Thunder rolled like the blast of distant cannon fire until an unusually loud clap startled their majesties and forced them to seek shelter.

At the same time on the plain opposite King Bela's fortress, a young messenger plodded across the wet sand to the tent of Kadan, the Tartar chief.

"I have been sent to you, Grand and Respectful Kadan," he said, bowing low, "by our people beyond the Carpathians, to tell you that the Great Khan, leader of all our tribes, is dead."

Such news, coming on the eve of battle, was to Kadan not only a great sorrow but an evil omen. He ordered the immediate breaking of camp, and he and his followers made haste to return to their homeland beyond the Carpathians in time for the burial service of the Great Khan.

For three days the rain continued to fall in such heavy sheets that King Bela's lookout men could not sight the opposite plain, but on the fourth morning when the queen awakened, the sun glinted through a crevice in the stone wall of the fortress. She called the king, and together they looked from the only window, high in the turret. Below them the sea lay blue and peaceful. Waves lapped the sandy edge of the plain where the flat-bottomed boats had been moored. A few gray storm clouds hung close over the horizon, but not a boat, nor a tent, nor a man could be seen. Only patches of charred ground showed that the Tartars had been there.

The king pondered the sight, not quite willing to believe his eyes. He questioned himself, saying, "It could be that the Tartars have merely withdrawn a pace to deceive us, or this could be some phenomenon of their wicked power.

It was not until later in the day that Bela knelt before his Creator and acknowledged His aid. This he did with the queen, and again they renewed their promise when Bela learned from some peasants whom the Tartars had over-taken in their flight and let go unharmed, the reason for the withdrawal. He declared a day of thanksgiving and ordered the solemn singing of the *Te Deum*, the ancient Christian hymn of praise.

But before talk of their merciful deliverance from the Tartars died on the lips of the people, a still greater day dawned.

Trumpets sounded to north and south and east and west in the Kingdom of Hungary. Messengers bearing royal arms urged their white horses to a faster pace. They rode from town to town announcing the birth of a royal child, Margaret, daughter of Bela the Fourth, and Maria Lascaris, the queen.

Inside the castle ladies-in-waiting tiptoed in and out of the nursery to look at the baby Margaret, asleep in her pearl-lined cradle.

"It is the same cradle," observed one elderly dame, "in which the great and holy Elizabeth of Thuringia slept. Great things should come of this child, too."

Among the nobles there was much speculation as to what would become of a princess whose parents had promised her to the service of God.

CHAPTER II

"Multos Annos"

ONE summer's day a few years later, some villagers who had gathered from round about the royal castle were exchanging the greeting "Praised be Jesus Christ," which was customary in that Christian country, when their salutations were interrupted by the rapid gallop of horses and the tinkling of bells. Before they had time to look, King Bela's courier rode by.

He leaned from his saddle, calling, "Clear the way, clear the way! The king returns in haste."

At the courier's words, fat white geese which had come to the edge of the road in search of a tastier worm waddled back to the fields. Not so the villagers. They moved to one side and took up their conversations, discussing the peace that had come in the last years of King Bela's reign.

"It's three years now since there has been any sign of war in our land," said a little man with a barrel-like stomach.

"That's right," agreed another. "And I have never before had such good crops."

"What day is today?" inquired a third man. "What is it that brings the king home in such great haste?"

A woman with a coif over her head hurried to the same side of the road. Hearing the man's question and being annoyed with his stupidity, she called to him, "You lout! With such peace abroad, how could you not know it is the Princess Margaret's birthday?" Then she boasted. "Indeed, I, the royal seamstress, have made a dress for her, of such fine silk and stitched in gold thread as never your eyes have seen."

She gave her wide, full skirts a swish and was prepared to walk on when she was routed and forced into the field by the king and his retinue. They came at such a pace that they left the villagers gaping and gasping and coughing in a whirl of dust.

Margaret and her brother, the Duke Stephen, laughed as they watched the peasants from the castle balcony. Soon they could see their father with the other nobles rounding the bend that led up the hill and into the courtyard. The children waved excitedly, and when the first horse cantered through the gates, Margaret began to jump up and down in delight.

Stephen, who was a few years older, stopped waving and laid a hand on his sister's shoulder.

"A princess should be dignified," he told her.

In the courtyard below, the king swung from his ivory saddle, flicked his horse on the nose with the end of his glove, and went up the stairs.

He took the children by the hand and led them into the large hall where the queen and nobles awaited them.

Cooks stood by the gleaming caldrons of soup that sim-mered in the open fireplace. Already the long wooden tables held the silver platters of venison and roast duck and the mounds of white goat's cheese.

"Did you see a boar, my lord?" Stephen asked his father, after the king had made the sign of the cross and they were all seated.

"Yes, my son. It was necessary for us to kill two of them that attacked us in the thickly wooded area near Vesperim."

"Vesperim," the little princess repeated in her father's exact accent. The king lifted her from her small chair be-side his and sat her on his knee. Her long blue silk dress, woven with golden thread, rustled against his metal girdle. A glance of approval which the queen was quick to see crossed his face.

"Yes, I have been at Vesperim. I made all haste to return for our daughter's birthday."

The king bent his wind-tanned face to the little princess and kissed her. As he did so, he drew from the pocket of his hunting jacket a white dove's feather which hung from a silver chain.

"For our dove and our peace," he said, fastening it around Margaret's neck and watching her little hands carefully smooth the soft white feather.

"Yes, I have been at Vesperim," he continued, talking directly to the queen. "I have talked with the good Mother Prioress. She knew, through the Dominican provincial and our other Dominican friends, of our promise to give Mar-garet to the service of God. She will be received when they think she is old enough."

"I am old. How old?" asked the princess impatiently, clapping her small hand against her father's. He pushed his chair back and lifted her onto a stool that had been placed at his right. Whereupon the nobles rose from the table, crying, "Hail, Margaret! Multos annos, bonos annos, plenos annos videat!" Thus they sang in the Latin tongue, the language of the court, wishing her many good and fruitful years on this, her third birthday.

"You are old, my little one," Bela smiled, "but not quite old enough to leave us. A half year more."

Margaret stood silent on the stool beside her father. She reached for the white dove's feather upon which she pressed a kiss, then waved it at the brilliant company of men and women.

CHAPTER III

To Vesperim

SOON it was summer, with the hot sun ripening the wheat to a field of waving gold. One day at mid-morning Margaret stood alone on the balcony, looking down at Stephen, who rode with his father through the courtyard gates. She watched till the red plume on Stephen's cap had become almost a speck as he crossed the last wheat field and took the turn toward the vineyards and the lake.

When he returned, Stephen said to his sister, "I have been to Vesperim. It is a town on many hills with fields beyond. There is a lake near by, just as there is here, only it is much bluer and much, much larger. It is the Balaton."

His eyes grew round as he told Margaret what he had seen: "Rabbits were in the meadows near the edge of the forest, and on the priory chimney storks were nesting. You'll like the priory. Mother Prioress has given my lord, the king, a present for you, a parchment initialed in gold and blue lettering, with notes of the psalms she is waiting to teach you. Father Paul, who rode with us, says that they are the music of Holy Mother Church."

Meanwhile Stephen munched at a piece of cake and continued to regale his sister with stories. Presently the queen came through the nursery, and just in time to hear the little princess beg, "Take me, Stephen. Take me on your horse to Vesperim."

Gathering the child into her arms, the queen spoke softly. "My dear one," she said, "you shall go! To the good nuns, there to learn the service of God. He gave you to us. Now it is time for us to give you to Him because we have promised."

So it was that Princess Margaret went to Vesperim. On the day of her arrival the birches and maples in the enclosure garden were bright with autumn's tinge. Sleek black grackles darted from tree to tree in an attempt to draw close to the chapel windows and blend their clipped chatter with the sweet-pitched voices of the nuns.

The ride had been an adventure. One of the horses had stumbled, losing his shoe, and almost caused the carriage to be jolted into a ditch. Emerging from the forest which lay about the castle they had come into open country. Women walked along the highway with covered baskets under their arms. Men drove pigs and yoked oxen. Margaret had never seen such a sight for never before had she been abroad on market day. When she asked her father why the pigs were not in the fields, he told her that their owners were taking them to market.

Then reflecting that his small daughter would not be likely to see such a day again, the king had ordered the carriage to draw up at the village square. Here the royal party stopped long enough to permit Margaret a hasty visit to the stalls.

When the princess climbed back into the carriage, laden with red apples which the Countess Olympiade, who accompanied her, had bought, she straightened herself against the silk cushions and began to feel along the sides for her parchment scroll.

"The songs I am going to learn for Mother Prioress," she had said when the queen had tucked the parchment in beside her little daughter.

"For God," the queen had corrected gently. "All that you do and learn at Vesperim must be for Him and for country. Try hard, my child. Be humble and brave, as befits the daughter of a king."

With her mother's words in her heart, Margaret entered the Dominican priory as though it were a second home. Mother Prioress, in white scapular and black cape, greeted the royal party, bowing first to the king, then to Margaret and the Countess Olympiade. The Prioress's cheeks, which were almost the color of the apples Margaret carried, dimpled when she saw that the princess had brought with her the parchment scroll. Margaret curtsied to the assembled nuns, who bowed a greeting in return.

The Prioress, who was neatly plump and very pleasant, invited Margaret and the Countess to see the priory. They walked down a long corridor that led to a stone-vaulted chapel. Here Mother Prioress placed a small kneeler in front of the altar in the Lady Chapel and beckoned Margaret to kneel on it.

"This is to be your place among us, Princess Margaret," smiled Mother Prioress, noticing the regal bearing of the tiny figure whose head barely reached to the top of the kneeler.

They walked on and went out into an open corridor. After the half-darkness of the chapel into which the sun's rays entered only through colored windows high in the nave, the little princess was blinded by the strong light. Mother Prioress bade her close her eyes for a moment, and when she

opened them, she saw two storks which circled overhead and then alighted with a swoop on the bakehouse chimney.

"It is just as Stephen said!" the princess told her father when they returned to the cloister parlor. "Tell him and my mother, and bring them to see me. I shall know how to sing when they come."

"Good-bye, my dove. Brave one, brave as any of the Arpad

family. I will bring her ladyship and Stephen after the fall rains."

The king signed his small daughter on the forehead with the sign of the cross and kissed her gently. Mother Prioress caught the sound of his lowered voice saying, "In this sign conquer," and it came from his lips as a prayer.

To the Countess Olympiade he said, "I am happy in knowing that the princess will be in your direct charge. Needless to say, the queen and I will miss you, and the court as well. We are indeed indebted to you for your services and those of your dear departed husband, the great Count Boriat. And now that you will be here at the priory with our daughter, it gives us comfort, for you knew the court as few do."

A deep curtsy was her only answer, but the king knew that his trust in her would never prove misplaced. He took leave with the words, "Dear Lady, I wish you God's peace in His service, and the same for the princess."

Shortly after Margaret's first meal at her priory home was over and her evening prayers said, she found herself wriggling contentedly in a straw pallet. It was firmer than the goose featherbed that had been hers at home in the castle, and it had a different scent about it too.

"It smells like the fields," she said to Countess Olympiade. "And cornflowers," she added, as an afterthought.

Then, remembering the blue of the flowers and that they were of the same color as the dress she had worn that day, she asked, "Will I wear the kind of dress as do the other children here?"

"Of course, dear princess, if you wish. But first, you must earn it." The countess moved across the room and bent over the bed to caress her precious charge. "Sleep in God's care," she whispered. "The morrow comes quickly."

But Margaret was already fast asleep.

CHAPTER IV

Lententide

"BENEDICAMUS Domino!"

"Benedicamus Domino, Sister Helen!"

The little princess threw back the homespun sheet and smiled up into the gentle face of the nun who had awakened her.

"You see, I remembered to say, 'Let us bless the Lord,' before anything else today," she said.

"You did indeed, Princess Margaret."

The child slipped her head through the white woolen dress made from the same material that the sisters wore, and which reached to her ankles, with a scapular of lighter

15

material over it. Sister Helen fastened the girdle that belted
the full skirt into place around the slim waist and pinned the
small white coif over her head. The coif let her brown curls
hang from under it, yet kept her hair clean. It was the
fashion, even in the cloisters of the day, to cover the heads
of small children.

"O ye sun and moon, bless the Lord! O ye stars of
heaven, bless the Lord!" gayly chanted the clear young voice
of the princess.

Sister Helen sighed. "Ah," she thought to herself, "what
enthusiasm the princess has!" It had not been so easy for
her, the Countess Olympiade, to throw off the manners of
the court and its comfortable ways for the rigors of the
priory, but it was not mere faithfulness to duty that urged
her on. No! "The love of Christ urgeth me on," she could
now truthfully say as she recalled those words from her
morning meditation.

Unaware of the thoughts her singing had caused, Margaret went about her dressing. She thrust her feet into
leather sandals, and her fingers grasped the rope thongs for
lacing. When she straightened up, she was facing the window. She saw the fields lying hard and fallow, with only
the gray glimmer of the sun to warm them.

"O ye mountains and hills, bless the Lord. O all ye things
that spring up in the earth bless the Lord ... "

Of a sudden she stopped singing and said, almost wist-
fully, "Spring will come soon."

"Your ladyship speaks full right. It is Lententide we are
biding. Your *fourth* Lententide in this holy house."

Margaret bethought herself of the stirrings of the birds
that would be coming to the garden, of the mother quail
leading her brood of young from under the bushes, and of
the swallows that nested under the chapel eaves. She re-

membered the nest she had been saving since last fall until the time when Stephen should visit her again.

At breakfast she continued to think of the things of spring—the apple orchard in bloom and the flowers she could gather to decorate the Lady Chapel.

"Marie Regnum," she said aloud, to the dismay of her companions, who ate in silence during the holy season of Lent.

But none of the elders took any notice of her remark, for Margaret was not only a princess, but also still among the youngest in the priory. Her poise drew the admiration of the nuns, and her gentle gay ways that of the children. When she laughed, it was like the musical sound of a brook, and they all loved to hear her.

However, her remark had not escaped Sister Helen, who wanted nothing less than perfection in her charge.

"Why spoke my princess of Marie Regnum at silence time?" she asked, when they were alone.

"I was thinking of Our Lady, whose kingdom this is. My father and mother have told me, and you have, too, Sister Helen, of how good King Stephen, my ancestor, gave this kingdom to Our Lady, Queen of Heaven, when he was dying, because his own son, Emeric, had been killed and he had no one to whom to leave it. You yourself said that King Stephen asked her motherly care for us, and that all Magyars, and I in particular, must thank Our Great Lady and ask her continued help. And, too, I was thinking of His Lordship, and when he will come again with my dear mother."

"I see, my child, that you are frank, and that you remember far too well. But come now, it is Lententide, and we must bethink us of the good Jesus who died for us."

Sister Helen repeated from memory the gospel narrative of Christ's passion and death. Margaret listened attentively but said little. When Sister Helen finished, the girl went as usual to join the other children in their play.

They assembled in the hall with the red flagstone floor. The day was damp and gray, so a fire of straw faggots had been lit, and the children seated themselves around it. Margaret's place on the center stool awaited her. Then the children began to sing. They passed a button on a thread from hand to hand in rapid fashion. When the singing ceased, it was Margaret's turn to guess who held the button.

"Agnes," she said, naming the correct holder, and the game continued until the children grew tired. Finally the older ones began to sew and the younger ones to draw. Margaret sorted through some colored papers and chose a specially bright red one. Then she left the room. She went so noiselessly that she was not missed until Mother Prioress and Sister Helen came looking for her. Not finding her, they went to the whitewashed alcove and drew back the starched linen curtains. They thought that perhaps she might have gone to sleep on her straw pallet.

"The old ewe has a new lamb," Sister Helen remarked thoughtfully. "The princess might have gone down to see how they fared, or to the farmer's child who lies sick."

Sister Helen offered to go in search of the missing child, and Mother Prioress started back to her duties. On her way she entered the Lady Chapel. .

The smell of wax hung heavy in the air, and the light from a single candle burned steadily. Its glow enabled the Prioress to see the shadowy outlines of a figure prone on the altar steps. As she drew near she distinguished the crucifix above the altar, which the candle lighted, and the figure of a child who lay with arms outstretched in the form of the

cross. She heard a sobbing voice murmur over and over, "My Lord Jesus. Me, too. Let me too suffer."

Quietly the Prioress withdrew from the Chapel. She met Sister Helen hurrying through the open corridor.

"Mother Prioress! Oh, Mother Prioress, please excuse me. I have sought the princess, but she is not to be found. Sister Cunegunde tells me that the farmer offered her a new kitten when she went to see how the ewe and the lamb fared, but she refused, although I had thought she wanted one. And she is not with the sick child, either."

Mother Prioress, who had listened calmly, slowly shook her head and then nodded it toward the Chapel. *"It seems to me God teaches our little princess His ways this Lententide."*

With that she was gone, leaving Sister Helen to discover for herself the meaning.

CHAPTER V

The King's Visit

ALL spring Margaret followed after the two lay sisters, Sister Maria and Sister Tilda. She went with them to the wash house and carried the wooden buckets to the well for filling.

The days grew warm, and the child would have liked to linger at the well long enough to take off her sandals, spill the cool, fresh water down between her toes, and then walk with wet feet on the grass.

"But," she thought, "I must hurry if I would learn all the tasks of the Priory."

"Not a drop wasted, and not a drop more could you have put in those buckets, my lady. The wool should come white with this last washing," said Sister Maria when Margaret put down the buckets on the wash house floor and tried to balance herself without staggering.

Sister Maria lifted the buckets over the fire while Margaret sorted the wool into piles. The burrs held fast in the mud-caked fleece scratched her hands as she sorted. She lifted an armful of wool over the vat. Steam melted the grease in the wool and sent it running down her arms in thick yellow streaks.

Sister Tilda stopped cording to wipe the sweat from her face. She frowned at Margaret.

"Mother Prioress likes it not that you spend such long hours here. This is no task for a princess."

"But if the princess wished not to be a princess," said the child, "but only the servant of the Lord, King of heaven and earth?"

"How now, your ladyship? You are the daughter of a king. Trouble not. God ordains what falls out for each of us."

"And you are no fit sight for a king," added Sister Maria, who was only half listening to what was being said and did not dream that Margaret spoke of other than her own father. "Go change your clothing. I have heard talk that Father Paul is expected this way on Corpus Christi."

"Maybe he is coming from the Cummanian mission he told us about," said Margaret, her eyes lighting at the thought.

"Never mind, child, where he comes from. He could come today, and your ladyship is no fit sight."

Margaret looked down at her grease-stained apron. The odor of wet wool hung about her. "The Sisters are right," she thought. "Father Paul could come today." With a quick smile of assent toward Sister Maria she laid aside her work and left the wash house.

She crossed the short meadow that lay between the Priory and the outer buildings. She was rounding the scullery hall when she heard men's voices.

"You have ridden hard, son. Your horse's withers give you away. It was not a short cut you took."

It was her father speaking, and then, as she darted upstairs, she heard Father Paul say laughingly, "Maybe he took the long road in search of a Cummanian princess, my lord, and a pretty one at that."

Upstairs Margaret could hear them ringing the portress's bell. There was not time for heating wash water. In her alcove she filled the basin with cold water from the pitcher and scrubbed as best she could, but sheep lanolin was not easy to remove.

She heard the squeaking of leather and new sandals in the cloister corridor, and Sister Helen drew back the curtains of the alcove.

"His Lordship is here with Father Paul and the Duke Stephen. Your queenly mother was none too well, so they did not bring her. They have not come by carriage."

Sister Helen's cheeks were flushed with excitement over the royal visit. So elated was she that she did not take note of her charge until she saw her in the cloister parlor beside Duke Stephen, flicking away some dust that clung to his doublet. The girl's fingers were stained, and yellow grease soiled her white woolen habit.

The princess sat talking with Stephen while Sister Helen chatted with King Bela and Father Paul. However, the girl was aware that the eyes not only of Sister Helen, but also of her father, were on her hands and the spots on her white habit. She recalled Sister Tilda's words, "No fit task for a princess," and her own reply, "I only wish to be the servant of the Lord, King of heaven and earth."

Father Paul, the Dominican Prior, a stooped, gaunt man who had come to Hungary with a band of his followers at the king's request to work among the Cummanians and other pagans living in the outlying parts of the Christian kingdom, smiled at the princess when she shifted uneasily and tossed her curls back from her shoulders.

"Your ladyship is big enough to be getting into things." he said. "What have you been about today?"

"I have had such fun, a whole springtime of fun!" replied the princess. And she told them about the ewe and the lambs and the shearing.

"Your Lordship, the princess wills to learn all the tasks of the Priory, and she cries when I restrain her," Sister Helen said by way of excuse.

The king replied. "Well . . . let her, if she enjoys it. It is seemly that a princess should weave and embroider and learn the language of the court and the ways of her people and how to pray well." "But," he added, looking again at the soiled hands and clothing of the girl, "one day of this should be enough, let alone a whole springtime."

"Excuse me, my lord, but you have forgotten the ring," Stephen interrupted in a effort to save his sister further embarrassment. "And you said that you wished to talk with Mother Prioress alone."

The king reached into the inner pocket of his purple tunic and drew from it a packet which he handed to Stephen for his sister.

"Show Margaret your new mount, and you had better have one of the hostlers wipe dry the mare's withers," he said. Then, remembering that there were no hostlers at the priory, he added, "Maybe one of the farmer's lads will tend to it."

Then he turned remorsefully to Margaret. "And see, my dove. The ring her ladyship sends you she designed to sparkle on the soft white hand of a princess and to cast rainbows on her weavings, as becomes the first daughter of the land." There was a note of majesty and regal pride in King Bela's voice, stronger than Margaret had ever heard before. Especially when he said, "You are of the royal family of Arpad, remember, and the princess!"

That evening, when Sister Helen came to summon Margaret to Compline, the night prayer of the Priory, she found her sorting the possessions which she kept in a chest beside her straw pallet. Sitting in one corner was a carved wooden doll in the dress of a Tartar maid. Margaret was talking to it as she braided its black shining hair.

"With God's help," she said, "Father Paul will teach you

it is wrong to burn our lands and kill our people."

She put the doll aside and lifted a bundle of sharp thistles from the chest.

Sister Helen watched in silent amazement.

"Of all things to save," she thought. "I will see about this. Of course, I have seen the peasants with their rough, coarse hands, using them for scrubbing."

The next day Father Paul, followed by the sisters in their black capes, the novices with their white veils, and the children of the Priory walked in the Corpus Christi procession through the enclosure garden and across the farmlands to the very edge of the forest. They sang as they walked, and their voices carried to the tree tops and to the blue summer sky.

Margaret walked behind the farmer lad who swung the censer filled with burning incense, and quite close to Father Paul. She strewed red petals from the poppies she carried, and white field daisies, praying that there might be enough bread in the land for all. As she plucked at the flowers, one could see that her hands were clean, but scratched red as the poppy petals, and no ring on her finger caught the gleam of the June sun.

On the contrary, Father Paul had gone to the Prioress, holding the ring in his hand. "She begged so hard," he said, "that I could not refuse her. She is asking that I use it for church vessels in the new Cummanian mission, and she gave me a handful of gold coins that Duke Stephen had given her, to use for my poor."

"She is a tender-hearted child," said Mother Prioress.

"Indeed, she is," agreed the priest, "but don't you think that she should have more time for play? She is so earnest. Let her play with the farmer lad, too. I am certain it will not hurt her any."

CHAPTER VI

The King's Gift

"WHAT said the king?"

Mother Prioress and her counsellors were assembled in the chapter room, where the nuns gathered to discuss their business affairs and confess their faults.

"His lordship spoke of serious things, serious for us," returned the Prioress. "I had thought to tell him of Princess Margaret's request. Of course you know, dear sisters, that she has asked to be admitted to our order. Father Paul agrees that she has an understanding beyond her years. However, I have ordered her more time for play, according to his suggestion. If in two years she understands the full meaning of King Bela's promise and desires to serve her people by offering her life in this way, then she may become a novice."

Then, returning to the original question the counsellors had asked, the Mother Prioress, looking more portly than

ever, continued, "His Majesty spoke to me of his plans. The
court is moving to Buda. It is a more strategic point. The
boats can ply the Duna to the east and west, and past many
of the new fortresses the nobles are building along its
course. Besides, the king thinks it better to have access to
the nobles in the western part of the kingdom in case of
attack. King Bela spoke of the rich land that is now being

worked by yeomen called Walloons, whom he encouraged to
migrate here from Flanders. They are skilled in farming.
The king says they have already cleared the fields, and there
are great stretches of grain and grazing lands that do not
lend themselves to the planting of vineyards such as we
have here."

The nun went on at length in her account of the king's
talk. Then, noticing the strained though polite face of Sister Hedwig, which indicated that the latter was anxious to

be about other things, the Mother Prioress came to the point.

"Yes, Sisters, directly below the new royal fortress in Buda, the king says there is a wooded island, a paradise for bird and beast. It is uninhabited. Large hares—you have all seen them, and you, Sister Tilda, know their ravages in the lettuce patch—abound there. I pray they will not cause us difficulties. It is called Hare Island, but the king thinks to call it Margaret Island and to build there a new priory for us in honor of the princess.

"When I told His Majesty of her request to join us, he said, with no small degree of pride, 'The first Arpad to serve God as a nun! He has ratified our promise in her. May He accept her offering of herself. All the women of the kingdom will look to her.' "

Mother Prioress cleared her throat and then went on. "Sister Helen, seven of us will go for the new foundation, which will be ready in two years."

"And did you wish to tell me, Mother Prioress, that the princess will spend a few days in court before going to the new foundation?" asked Sister Helen quietly.

Mother Prioress lifted her eyebrows and ignored the question. She finished her discourse by saying, "The child will know better in two years what calling the court has for her."

CHAPTER VII

Trouble in the Kingdom

THE hot summer sun browned the face and hands of the princess as she strode through the open fields with Jansci, the head farmer's youngest son. With him, she gathered the freshly cut wheat into bundles. Often the children paused to play hide-and-seek behind the stacks. Again, Margaret would take the threshing flail and amuse Jansci with blundering strokes that merely cut the air. These days she wore no coif on her head. She had asked to keep it uncovered as Jansci did and was granted permission because Sister Maria had remarked that she was growing too fast and was too pale. Sister Helen had shortened her habit and given her a thinner garment.

Once a week during the warm days, Sister Helen took the Priory children to the stream that ran through the farthest meadow of the enclosure. This day Jansci was the first to wade into the clear water.

"Look how Our Heavenly Father feedeth us," said Margaret, savoring a handful of watercress that grew by the edge. Agnes, also a child of noble birth, hopped from stone to stone. She was stooping to turn one over when Jansci swung a small crab onto the bank. He made such an outlandish remark that Sister Helen forbade him to repeat it.

"You are as shrill as a shrew, Jansci," she said.

"What is a shrew?" Jansci wondered. "Something not very nice, anyway."

Hearing Sister Helen's remarks, Margaret recalled Stephen's usual comments when his horse's stirrup slipped or he missed his aim in shooting. Jansci's words were not so different. Moreover, he had shown her how to slide in the hay, and where the meadow larks nested.

"Jansci," said the princess, "did you ever hear this? 'O ye whales and all that move in the waters, bless the Lord! O all ye fowls of the air, bless the Lord!' "

Jansci wriggled his toes on the sandy bottom of the stream.

"Crabs can bless the Lord as well as whales, even if they pinch," Margaret continued, and the other children pondered the truth of her statement.

On the way home, they saw lavender blooming amidst the dry meadow grass.

"Pick some, Jansci," said Margaret.

The boy paused in the pealing of a reed. "What for, your ladyship?"

"To put between clean linens. It's as nice as incense," the princess said temptingly, knowing his great delight in swinging the church censer and watch the pungent vapor ascend into the air.

The farmer's son eyed his coarse brown jerkin, then stretching his hand toward a stalk of the blue tassled flower he stooped down and cut it close to the ground. Margaret was amused as she watched him rubbing it against himself.

"It's not done like that," she laughed. "The perfume will not last. By Christmas time, after it has lain in the sun and dried, it will be ready. I'll bring you some then if you will help me gather it."

Along the tow path to the right, doors of houses stood ajar. Flies flew freely in and out, and a pig grunted his way in just as freely. Sometimes he was noisily shunted to the pen at the side of the cluster of huts that made up the farmers' quarters. These people were peasants who worked and tilled the soil for the nuns of the Priory and, in return, had farm lands of their own to work and a small share of the Priory crops.

Sister Helen attempted to hurry the children along, but this day the princess would not be hurried. She peered into every open door, without exactly staring. The unpleasant smell of the houses, the dirt floors, and the dust that rose from the stale rushes troubled her.

"Do you think lavender would help?" she asked Sister Helen.

"Lavender could, your ladyship, but I fear it is a problem of customs and manners more than smells." The nun slackened her pace into a more thoughtful gait. "It is not easy to change the ways of a Nomad people. It takes patience and schooling in the habits of cleanliness and love for a fixed abode. Too, many there are who think knowledge and cleanliness only for the few."

"But what is our thought?" Agnes interrupted, speaking in the manner of the nuns, who used the plural because they never wished to feel a personal ownership even in something as small or as big as an opinion. Then, not giving Sister Helen an opportunity to reply, Agnes went on talking, "My father says it is enough to try to teach the roving Cummanians our ways, and that the nobles are angry because. . ."

"Because the king has asked the cooperation of the Cummanians, knowing what it means to have their support should the Tartars again invade the land. Besides, he is a man desirous of peace." Sister Helen completed the sentence over which Agnes, suddenly conscious of the presence of the princess, had hesitated.

By this time they had reached the Priory and there was no further discussion. The children had sniffed the fragrance of fresh bread as they filed through the scullery and their attention was now fixed on the table where Sister Tilda had spread a supper of thick slices of dark brown bread, jam, milk, and a special treat of fresh peaches sent by one of the nobles.

Margaret barely touched the food, and went directly afterwards to the chapel and then to bed. She lay wakeful. Never had the time between Compline and Matins, the late prayer which was said at midnight, seemed so long to the princess as on this night. .

She knew that Sister Helen often spent the entire time between the recitation of these two prayers in the chapel. But with the long walk and the heat of the day surely she should come to bed early this once.

Finally, there was the creaking of the door, and the linen curtains of the alcove were drawn aside. In the moonlight, Sister Helen put off her wimple, and beside it she placed her cowl. Something dark and thickly wadded lay next to her skin. This she drew around her body and tucked firmly under the cincture with which she girded herself.

Margaret turned on her side facing the wall. The meadow, the stream, Jansci flinging away the crab, all passed before her. She turned onto her other side. This time Agnes's words echoed within her. She had tried to forget them when she was eating her supper and when she had gone to chapel. She turned a third time, and her straw pallet rustled beneath her.

At the sound Sister Helen turned and came toward the bed of the princess. "Ave," she said, using the greeting she would have spoken to one of the nuns. It was the time of the great silence when one spoke only out of necessity and then only in a whisper. She leaned over close to the princess and asked, "What disturbs your ladyship that you turn so frequently and sleep not? Are you ill?"

"Oh, no," the princess whispered back, flinging her arms about Sister Helen's waist, only to pull them away quickly and rub them because of the prickling. Margaret shivered. "Is it a hair shirt, Sister Helen? A hair shirt of nettles?"

"Yes, but it is only for God to see, my princess, and only on rare occasions do I wear it. Now, tell me, what ails your ladyship, if you are not ill?"

"Agnes spoke today of the nobles and the Cummanians. The nobles are angry with his lordship, my father, because he would protect the Cummanians. Things are not well in the kingdom. You cannot hide it from me."

"Make not overmuch of gossip and misunderstanding, child. The king's policy is a wise one. In time God will manifest it."

"Sister Helen," whispered the princess, pressing both hands against the nun's chest and this time making no effort to withdraw them, "you wear the hair shirt as a penance so that God may have mercy on you?"

"You speak truly," came the humble admission.

"Then I shall wear a hair shirt that God may have mercy on our people."

Sister Helen wanted to object to such a measure but, even as the words of protest formed in her mind, the princess lay back on the straw pallet and fell asleep in the peace of her determination.

CHAPTER VIII

Margaret's Secret

O N Christmas Day Margaret seated herself below the
salt at table, a place reserved for those of lower sta-
tion by the custom of mediaeval great folk who de-
sired their most distinguished guests to sit in the
highest places and season the dinner with their company.
In short, the placement of the salt at table regulated the
seating of the guests. But despite the fact that the princess
had sought a lower place for herself, a great silver platter
was set before her and she was bidden to serve herself even
before Mother Prioress.

It was then that she said, "I know of only one thing in
the world which makes me sad."

Those serving her wondered what it could be that could
cause sadness on such a day of general rejoicing.

The princess picked up her plate and moved to the vacant
chair at the greatest distance below the salt. "I wish I had
been born in a thatched hut in some far away village, instead of a castle. Then I should be worth only what I am in
myself, and not what I owe to my parents."

37

"You may have your wish, at least in part," Agnes remarked sharply. "Haven't you heard, your ladyship, that the Tartars are again encamped in the Carpathians?" As she spoke, she cast a frightened look around at the other children who had remained at the Priory for the feast. There had been a heavy rain and a sudden blanket of snow, which made the roads impassable. The girl's fear spread to the children, who had heard tales of the burning and pillaging done by the Tartars.

"If they came and took us, I could live in one of their ugly tents," retorted the princess.

"But they might hold you as a hostage, or marry you," Agnes said, forgetting her fear.

"I would cut off my nose, and they would not want me."

Sister Helen's hand rested on the shoulder of the princess. "Children, children, on the feast of the Holy Child to talk of such calamities!"

Seeing that their plates were emptied, Sister Helen suggested that they go into the hall and play hoodman's blind, a game similar to blindman's bluff.

"Later in the afternoon, when the wind has quieted down, we shall take our gifts to the peasants," she promised. "And Princess Margaret, you have the ribbons to make ready your gift for Jansci."

Margaret went at once to get Jansci's gift and the ribbons for tying it, and as she returned she was met by Mother Prioress, who stood just outside the door, admiring the firm light step with which the princess approached her.

"What soft garment have you there, your ladyship?" questioned the Prioress.

Sister Maria, passing by, recognized the rough brown material she had assisted Margaret in weaving. Just then the material slipped from under the princess's arm, and to her confusion she saw that it was not the soft brown jerkin she had made for Jansci and had folded with lavender. *It was her own new hair shirt!*

"Dear child, certainly you had not in mind such a gift for anyone on the feast of the Divine Child, had you? It is so unlike your ladyship. This is a rough garment, bound with sackcloth." Mother Prioress took hold of it and ran her fingers over the coarse edges.

"No ... no, Mother Prioress, that is the wrong garment," answered the girl.

"But whose is it?" asked Mother Prioress. "To whom does it belong?"

"To Margaret Arpad," came the unhesitating answer, and with that the princess, making use of her right to command —a right reserved to the highest in the land and one she had never used before—reached out her hand and took back the garment. "Excuse me, Mother Prioress, but the princess has need of it."

In the great hall where the children played, Sister Maria told Sister Helen about the scene that had taken place in the corridor. "I helped her ladyship with the weaving of the coarse material," she confessed, "but I had not thought as to what she would do with it. Her ladyship said it was a secret."

"Nothing awry, Sister Maria," Sister Helen comforted the lay sister. "It is well to remember that the princess's lineage is one of heroes and saints. Stephen, our first great king, and Emeric, his son, and now Elizabeth of Thuringia, her aunt. All Bavaria speaks of her and honors her. Besides, the princess has heard much of the ways of martyrs here."

Mother Prioress had joined them before Sister Helen finished speaking, and she said sternly, "It may be well,

Sister, but a hair shirt is not a garment for a child, and it is not becoming to make a jest of holy discipline. Moreover, the princess's grandfather, Andreas II, was given to such extremes as were never known throughout Europe. Have you forgotten the golden bathtub he sent to Bavaria as part of Elizabeth's trousseau? God rest his soul, but it is not good to foster these extremes in the princess."

Sister Helen stood up, partially out of politeness and partially to control her anger. After all, had she not spent her early years in the court of Andreas II, and had she not seen both the great excesses and the penances of the king?

"It was never my intent, Mother Prioress, to make a mockery of discipline as we understand it among nuns. It is true there may have been extremists among the princess's ancestors, but the greater number were men and women of virtue and courage."

"I myself gave the princess her first hair shirt. It did not occur to me to seek further advice. For many months the princess has fretted over the conditions in the kingdom. She has spoken of the extravagances of the nobles and their constant quarreling with his lordship, her father, and she puzzles over the neglect of the poor.

"Mother Prioress, the princess came upon a hair shirt quite by accident, and knowing it to be a garment worn in penance, she has asked whether she might wear one for the sins of her countrymen. At first, I, too, thought it a passing fancy, and I dared to indulge it."

Sister Helen suddenly dropped to her knees before Mother Prioress, and there were tears in her eyes.

"I feared the princess might fall ill," she said, "and I took back the hair shirt which she wore almost constantly. Now you see, Reverend Mother, she has made one for herself more coarse than anything I had given to her."

CHAPTER IX

The Princess at Court

"MARGARET! Princess Margaret Arpad!" The children's voices were filled with excitement and were unusually loud for those of Priory children. "The carriages are here! Two of them!"

Their words reached Margaret kneeling in the Lady chapel. Slowly she closed the door behind her and walked into the open, where bundles were already being loaded into the carriages. She was opening and closing her hands as she walked, as though she would hold in something and then let it go.

At the sight of her, the coachmen dropped what they were carrying and bent low, recognizing her as the princess by her spirit and the lofty way she carried herself. Mother Prioress bustled about giving orders, as usual.

"Now, in regard to the carrying of the altar vessels for

the new chapel," she said, "these, Sister Helen, are to be taken in the carriage with you."

The children gathered around the princess, and Agnes spoke the thought held by all.

"Your ladyship in Priory dress! You are going home to court like that!"

They were visibly disappointed, for they had looked forward to seeing the princess dressed as they thought she should be.

"This is the dress that marks me as the servant of my people," said Margaret.

"At the court," Agnes insisted, "surely you will not wear it."

Margaret smiled and made no reply. All the sisters of the Priory looked on, some with handkerchiefs wiping the tears from their eyes, for it was not likely that they would again see the little princess who had grown up in their midst, or the two Sisters leaving with her for the new foundation on Hare Island.

Jansci stood among the men. He held a bouquet of blue cornflowers and white daisies. He bent and kissed the hand of the princess as he had seen great men do. He did not say good-bye when he gave her the flowers, which are considered by all Hungarians to be the loveliest in their land since they grow in their fertile plains. Without looking back, the lad walked toward the meadows at the rear of the Priory.

With great dignity Mother Prioress gave her blessing to the two Sisters and the princess, and then the two carriages wound their way out of the enclosure garden, much as a funeral procession would do. In the first carriage, Sister Helen rode with the princess and Sister Maria. The wheels rumbled over the ruts in the road. In places muddy pools

of water filled the road, and the horses had to lunge and
strain and splash their way to surer ground. They had gone
but a few miles when two horsemen came up to the window
of the first carriage. Hearing their approach, the princess
drew aside the curtain.

"Father Paul! Jansci!" she exclaimed.

"Ah, your ladyship, surprise indeed! At King Bela's request, we are going to accompany you to the court, and I will
remain there until after the official opening of the new
Priory."

"But Jansci!"

"Yes, Jansci, too. Speak for yourself, lad," said the priest.

Jansci reined his horse tighter in order to check its splashing into a puddle in the road.

"I had asked Father Paul to take me with him to his monastery," he explained, "but as I know only the things of the fields and stables, I thought I could serve the glory of God by going along with Father Paul and caring for his horses when he is on mission. Now Father Paul has come for me. Master Hubert sent word a week ago. I am to be a lay brother."

"Jansci," said the princess with glowing eyes, "I dared hope such for you."

"But you," Jansci chided, remembering the days when they had played together and the princess had told him how her parents had consecrated her to the service of God and her people, and that she wished to remain at the Priory forever, "but you, your ladyship, may find the court more to your liking than the Priory, and think to stay."

The lad peered more deeply into the brown eyes of his former playmate.

"Look for me on Hare's Island," said the princess. "Ask Father Paul to bring you on my vow day, the day that I of my own choice shall be no longer Margaret, Princess of the house of Arpad, but simply Margaret."

Father Paul spurred his horse and prepared to move ahead of the carriages, and Jansci followed. He caught a last glimpse of the princess fastening the carriage window closed.

"Closed," thought Jansci, "closed."

It was late evening when the horses made their way up the steep hills of Buda and into the courtyard. Stable lackeys loitered there, holding torches that had been dipped in pitch and gave off a blazing light.

"Isten Hostem! God give you welcome," they said when they swung open the doors of the carriage before the coachmen could dismount.

Duke Stephen was the first of the royal household to greet his sister.

"I've a mind to carry you in. You look tired after the journey, but you've grown taller."

"So have you, Stephen," said the princess, eyeing her brother, who wore the crest of Arpad embroidered into his fur-lined cape.

"And Sister Helen Olympiade," said the young duke. "The widow of the great Count Boriat. It is a joy to welcome you to court again, however brief the stay."

"And Sister Maria," the princess said, presenting the lay sister to her brother.

Ladies in waiting thronged the halls. Nobles in striped cloaks rose from their tables of chess, and pages stood at attention as Duke Stephen, with the princess and the two nuns, made a quiet entry and went directly to the king's quarters.

Soon the court buzzed. The princess would dine in private with her father and mother. Bela had not recovered from a heavy cold that had kept him confined in his own quarters most of the winter.

In still another quarter a young squire from the French court, where Duke Stephen had visited, twitted him. "Her ladyship, your sister, is comely," he said. "And quite a picture in her Priory dress. Methinks she has much courage, and I'll wager she'll like the court. I take it her ladyship rides."

"Princess Margaret has lived at the Priory in Vesperim most of her childhood," the duke answered by way of explaining his sister's lack of courtly aptitude.

"But I'll wager she'll soon ride, and well. With her natural grace she should sit a saddle well." The tall young squire bent down to adjust the orange tips of his boots, which had a tendency to crinkle. When he looked up, a curly-headed page in red and gold velvet was making his way with a huge tray on his arm to the king's quarters.

"That reminds me," the squire continued, "that page, who behaves like a perfect prig, reported in other quarters that her ladyship had not come, and I would have believed him, had I not seen and recognized the lovely Princess Margaret myself. The boy said that only three Sisters, one much younger than the others, got down from the carriage. The stupid fellow! Next he will be reporting as truth the rumor that Boleslas of Poland has asked for and won her hand."

"Boleslas may have asked," the Duke replied, "but the winning—ha, now!"

CHAPTER X

Stephen Wins A Wager

DUKE Stephen drew aside the curtains of his sister's quarters. "I thought I would be the first to greet you on your first morning home, but I see that my queenly mother is ahead of me. I wish you the greetings of the day, sweet mother, and you, fair Princess Margaret.

He turned again to the queen. "Did you show her ladyship the gold-embroidered dress, the gift of the Cummanian princess, and the other gifts from all over the realm and France and Germany?"

"Not yet, my son. We have been looking down on Hare's Island. Margaret wondered if we could see the new Priory from here. Already she is lonely for her cloister and anxious to go there."

"To go there! Today, my queenly mother! I have a wager with the French squire and some of the others that the princess can ride. I've ordered a gentle mount saddled for her. We could make it to the Priory together, and at the foot of the hill, before ferrying across, we could tether the horses and rest."

"Ride!" The princess looked in bewilderment first at Maria Lascaris, the queen, and then at her brother. "But it hardly suits me."

She shook the skirt of her habit, which fell in long graceful folds and all but hid her sandalled feet, then held it out wide.

"Margitka," said Stephen, addressing his sister by her pet name of nursery days, "you would be glad to mount and ride if the Tartars came and you had to flee for your life."

"Have you forgotten, Stephen, that the princess is God's gift of peace to our realm? Why frighten her with ideas of fleeing? Teach her to ride if you will, and she so desires. Do you, my child?" Maria Lascaris smoothed the princess's scapular and hugged her warmly.

"To the Priory," said the princess. "But my habit is not quite fit for riding."

"There should be a riding dress in the princess's wardrobe. I am certain that I saw one among her gifts," said Stephen, walking to the other end of the room and opening a huge carved chest. He held up, one by one, garments of velvet bound in fur, dresses and cloaks, and finally a green riding dress. At all these the princess looked admiringly, closely examining the handwork, until it came to putting them on. Then she begged to be excused from wearing even the riding dress, and choose instead to chance the ride in her priory habit.

She pinned her unruly curls up under her coif and went along happily with Stephen. Hand in hand, they made their way through the many rooms of the court, in and out, to the stables. Nobles and ladies paused in their activities and sought to engage the princess in conversation.

"Father Paul tells us," remarked a noble who spent most of his time poring over musty Latin documents, "that your ladyship has memorized the whole of the Psaltery."

"But, my dear," protested his wife, "the princess prefers to think of new and gay things like the minstrels tonight, or the jewels in her mother's crown."

"The princess is now going to ride with me. Our horses are ready," interrupted the duke, seeing the eagerness of the court for his sister's company. As they passed on, men put down their long Turkish pipes or drew a little more heavily on them, remarking, "She's as fresh as a morning rose."

"But a bit headstrong," observed an elderly lady, fussing at a loose thread in the tapestry on which she worked. (Her husband was one who always quarreled with the king.) "It was the queen's idea that the princess should appear in court in Priory dress, although I think the princess fancies the distinction herself. I can't say that I think it in good taste."

Count Ladislaw pulled at his mustache and chuckled, glancing around the assembled group. "From the accounts of Countess Olympiade," he said, "—excuse me, I mean Sister Helen—I think the idea the princess's own. It's good to see a lady, even a very young one, who dares to be different."

Silence fell among the ladies as though they had been suddenly ducked in cold water and had not breath to sputter.

Meanwhile Margaret and her brother reached the stables where the horses were waiting, ready for the morning's ride.

"If this soils," the princess told him, as she lifted her white robe above the sandals and he assisted her to mount, "it can be washed. Besides it is, in a particular way, mine."

"Quite so," Stephen agreed. "But there could be another plan for you, such as marriage, which might serve the **good**

of the kingdom and the people just as well as your spending
the rest of your days in a convent."

"Why, Stephen, one would think you knew nothing of the
nature of the vow to which their majesties pledged me. It
was a solemn promise made to God." The princess pressed
her heels against the horse's side and straightened herself
in the saddle, tucking her skirts under her.

"It was only a thought I've had ever since I heard that
Boleslas asked for your hand. But let us think no more of
it." And yet Stephen felt sure that if Margaret really loved
someone, she would feel differently about their parents'
promise.

"I say," he exclaimed with a certain feeling of pride, "you
sit as if you had ridden all your life!"

"I've watched others ride, thought not so many ladies,"
the princess said, flushing at his approval. "Even you, the
first time you came to Vesperim. Don't you remember?"

"Vesperim! And today it's another Priory you wish me
to take you to. His lordship says this one is to be your own.
Now, let out the reins, Margaret, or the horse will slip on
this steep grade. The carriage is taking Sister Helen and
Sister Maria at noon. We may meet them there."

In a valley between several hills Margaret dismounted and
leaned against an elm. The Danube was little more than a
hand's reach from where she stood, and now green and
grassy Hare's Island lay in full view, with the gray stone
walls of the Priory breaking the line of foliage against the
sky.

"Oh, I hope there is never a bridge to the island—just
little boats," the princess said.

"But that's not practical. It will be hard on the few
farmers' families living on the island who care for the
Priory, and on all who have any business there," Stephen

answered. "But his lordship says he has left it so for now on the advice of the Master General of the Dominicans and at Mother Prioress's request."

"And my own. Seeing the court makes me wish to be alone and forgotten." The princess traced the pattern in her brother's silken doublet with a wisp of grass. "Is the court always so gay, Stephen?"

"Often more so. Princess Margaret Arpad, I would inform you that the royal court of the Magyars has hardly an equal throughout Europe. There are more silks and tapestries and furs here than anywhere else, to say nothing of the gold vessels from the East. Our splendor is almost enviable. In France it was not so gay as here last winter. And though the cooking there was good, such a lack of flavor! Our kingdom is a Mecca, and in spite of our defeats we have risen. The world knows we are a bulwark against the Tartars."

"And the poor?" asked Margaret. "Were they the same as here, crowded into little huts?"

"I didn't see much of them. I was kept busy with my studies of the government, and then there were the minstrels, and I learned to play the flute. I visited the poor once a year, according to court custom, and I sent regularly more than an ample share of alms."

"And is it the custom of the French court to pray?"

"Pray?" said Stephen. "Well, yes. They had a royal chaplain, a likable man, but not so jovial as Father Paul or Master John or Father Marcellus, who I hear have won special favor with you."

"Yes," said Margaret, "for their gentle wisdom and goodness. They advise me well."

"Then I hope they will point out to you what is for the good of the Magyars, and the way you can best serve your people." The duke paused in the tethering of the horses before making ready to ferry his sister to the Priory. "It's been hard for the workmen, and slow, to carry the stones and all the material by boat to the island," he said, "even to the glass for the chapel windows."

That evening the duke remarked to his father, "I had a difficult time getting the princess home to court."

"She's just been here," Bela answered. "I told her that the flues in the chimney were not yet in order, and the entire Priory was still damp from the stonework, and it would be a few days before it would be livable."

"I told her the same, Your Lordship, but she wished to remain in spite of that. It was Sister Helen who persuaded her that it was her duty to spend a few more days in the court with Your Majesties, and that Mother Prioress had expressly ordered these holidays for her. Then she came like a lamb. Seeing her like that, one would never dream she was so wilful. She rode as if she'd always ridden, and she had no idea that the horse might shy or she be thrown. I think she enjoyed it."

The duke smiled at his father.

"Thanks to the princess," he went on, "I won my wager with Squire Philip. Not one of the squires or knights denies that the princess has spirit. And they find her bewitching and different in her white habit. Squire Philip mentioned something about Duke Boleslas asking for her hand. What happened, Your Lordship, may I ask?"

"My son, Boleslas is a good duke and a just man, and I have no doubt that such an alliance with Poland would have been for the good of our realm, but God seems to have ratified our promise in Margaret. A few years ago I spoke to her about going to Poland. She cried and begged to remain

at the Priory, and reminded your queenly mother and myself of our promise, so we took this as a sign."

The king shifted his position and eased himself back into
his chair. "This cold seems to have left me a bit stiff, and
my legs are swollen," he remarked. Then he looked search-
ingly at his son.

"Stephen, I have been quietly watching, and now it seems
well to tell you that the Cummanians, the king, his wife and
his daughter are welcome in this court, and it is not my in-
tention to restrict King Katony's orderings among his own.
However, it seems wise to request that you do not devote
yourself to the Cummanian princess or shower her with
your attentions. It would not be fitting. They are Chris-
tians, son, but our life and ways are new to them. We are
of a different lineage."

"Love goes deeper, Your Majesty." The young duke met
his father's eyes without blinking. "If King Katony will
consent to the marriage of his daughter to me, that is all I
ask."

"Take heed, my boy. Vipers are abroad, and in this very
court."

Bela lay back wearily. His hair silvered in the candle-
light, and the furrows of his brow deepened. He sighed,
"They could split this kingdom in two, such is their hate
for the Cummanians. With an effort he raised himself up
and his voice shook, almost pleading, "Mark me, son, take
heed! They will plot it if you make such a marriage."

CHAPTER XI

The Strange Knight

A LIGHT wind rustled the leaves into evening song and a star slid down the sky as Margaret, torch in hand, made her way to the hut where Sister Agnes lay with fever.

Margaret had volunteered to care for the sick of the priory, a task feared by most, because as often as not one could be stricken with what seemed only a fever but would be nothing other than the dreaded plague. And the plague spared not even those who sought to show mercy in nursing the victims.

But for Margaret nursing held no fear. It was all part of the service she had promised to God for the salvation of her people, the proud, haughty, and luxury-loving Magyars. It had been two years now since Bela the Fourth and his queen, Maria Lascaris, had knelt in the Priory they built for their daughter, and heard her in simple ceremony pronounce her vows as a Dominican nun.

Margaret tilted her head back and stopped for a moment to gaze at the stars. Suddenly she heard a low moan. Thinking Sister Agnes had grown worse, she hurried through the darkness, but as she neared the sister's hut, she discovered that the sound did not come from there, but down from the river.

The thought came to her almost as quickly as the sliding of the star that one of the farmers, coming home late, might have had a mishap with the boats. She ran through the low brush toward the bank. A white horse came neighing from behind a tree and cut across her path. There he stopped with his reins dangling from his silver bridle.

A nobleman's horse here on the island! Margaret had no time to think further, for the moaning sounds were clear and close. The horse trotted back through the dry brush, breaking and crackling it underfoot, and Margaret followed to where an armored knight lay on the ground, his leg caught under him and the white plume of his visor blown over his face. His horse stood beside him. Leaning toward the young knight, Margaret lifted back the visor from his sweat-covered face.

"Mi baj van?" she asked.

The knight opened his eyes, but made no answer.

"Mi baj van?" the princess asked again, and seeing that the knight's face twitched as he tried to speak, she realized that his physical pain might have been increased because he did not understand the Magyar tongue in which she had asked him what was the matter. She bent lower, and wiping his face with her handkerchief, spoke to him in Latin, for

if he were from any neighboring court, he should know that language.

"What is it, good knight, that ails you?" she asked. "And how come you hither?"

The knight pointed to the leg which was pinned under him. "I cannot move," he said. "I came hunting and slipped from my horse."

"Lie still, good knight. I shall go for the farmers, and we shall carry you on a board back to a vacant hut, a part of the cloister's infirmary. I shall care for you this night. It is beyond custom to disturb Mother Prioress so late."

Margaret bore a hole in the marshy earth by digging her heel back and forth. Into this she drove the birch-pitched torch she carried.

"This will give you comfort," she said, "and lead me back."

By starlight she groped her way to the Priory and the farmers' quarters and rapped loudly on the farmers' doors. She finally succeeded in rousing them and asking their aid. A greater part of the night she ran back and forth between the knight's hut and the Priory, fetching hot towels to poultice his leg and herb drinks to reduce his fever. In between times, she attended to Sister Agnes, who grew worse by the hour.

It was weeks later when the court of King Bela learned that a Bohemian knight had been visiting one of the Hungarian nobles, a dissenter from the court, at his castle a few miles east of Buda. The knight had gone hunting on Hare's Island, not knowing it was forbidden, and had fallen and injured himself. Princess Margaret had come upon him in the dark and had rescued him. Now there were rumors that the famed Ottokar, "Man of Iron," as he was called, the

King of Bohemia and the former enemy of Bela Fourth, had
heard stories from his knight of the beautiful nun who lived
in the Dominican Priory.

Soon afterward Ottokar, having decided to make peace
with King Bela, announced that he would pay him a visit.
The court speculated as to the true purpose of his coming.
"My dear," whispered the ladies one to another, "the peasants flock to the island. They believe that the princess has
found favor with God and has the gift of healing. And she
herself—have you seen her? It's ridiculous that any king
would seek peace by suing for her hand."

There was much nodding of heads and pursing of lips as
the whispers continued. "The princess is less than a serving
maid. She tends the sick and her clothes are in rags, always
patched at the knees from grovelling in the dust at her
prayers. She had the idea that she must offer herself in
this way. Preposterous, isn't it? It's no wonder we have
come to such a pass when the very highest in the land be-
have as though they had no pride or decency."

The men spoke more of political matters. "It is certainly
true that King Katony, the foxy fellow, with his following,
plotted to lag behind our men and pretend to lose their direction so as to join the Tartars in their recent sally on our men
in the Carpathians. The king did not wish to believe it, but
how could he be so blind? I am glad that the nobles forced
him to oust the Cummanians from the court. Duke Stephen
takes their part and is rallying the dissenting nobles for
war against his father. What can you expect? He married
that Cummanian without his father's consent!

Such was the talk that went on from day to day, until at
last it was reported that Ottokar had come in person, asking
Bela to take him to see the princess.

As they returned from the Priory Ottokar said: "Even
had my young knight not reported that it was as though a
creature from heaven looked down upon him when her ladyship ministered to him, I would have found her so myself.
I ask no dowry, King Bela. Only her love. I will give
Margaret the whole of my kingdom. Surely she cannot refuse when our marriage would unite two Christian peoples
and work to the good of both. She would be serving God as
well in such a manner."

He paused for a moment and then said thoughtfully, "I
will send to Rome myself, asking that she be released from
her vows. You, King Bela, must make the princess see this,
and ask the Dominicans, whose great benefactor you have
been, to assist you by their persuasion."

"I will try," promised Bela.

Days passed, and hour after hour King Bela and his
queen, Maria Lascaris, sat alone in their quarters, talking
over the proposal of Ottokar.

"We are harried by the dissenting nobles, and now this
civil war which Stephen has brought upon us," said the
king. "Such a marriage is a matter of statecraft," he
reasoned, "apart from gratifying the desires of King Ottokar."

His arguments failed to convince the queen. "Remember
our promise," she warned.

"But that was long ago. Conditions are different now.
We could not foresee what would happen. It is just as im-
portant that the princess give up her cloistered life for that
of the court of Ottokar. He is a good man and he loves her.
We Magyars need the strength of such an alliance."

Bela drew the queen into the circle of his arm and sought
reassurance in her eyes. "Ah, truly, the princess is our dove

and our peace. You, my beloved Maria, must point this out to her. Make her see that our views are now changed concerning that promise of long ago. And if the Holy Father says the vows are no longer valid because the princess made them in faithfulness to our promise, thinking she could best serve her people by dedicating her life to prayer and penance for the nation, then this will be a sign that all is well."

CHAPTER XII

The Promise Fulfilled

STILL as the earth before rain was the peace at Hare's Island. Margaret refused to see anyone coming from the court and took refuge in the chapel whenever she sighted any small craft plying the Danube in the direction of the Priory.

She had told the king and queen, when they had come to discuss the proposed marriage with King Ottokar, that she would never consent.

"I remember that when I was only seven you tried to espouse me to the Polish duke, now King Boleslas. And you remember the answer I gave you then. I told you that I wished to serve only Him to Whom you had consecrated me at birth. If then, when I was but a child, I would in no wise yield to your will in opposition to the claims of truth and justice, do you think that I am likely to give in to you now that I am older and wiser and more capable of grasping the greatness of my calling?"

She had remained unshaken in her determination and begged the king to relent. "Cease, then, my father, from trying to make me change my mind. For since I prefer the Heavenly Kingdom to that which has been offered to me by the King of Bohemia, so also do I prefer to die rather than obey this command of yours."

At this point, the queen, seeing that it was of no use to tempt the princess by the offer of earthly love and possessions, had seized upon her mention of obedience in a final plea.

"My child, are we not your parents? And does not the Gospel command you to reverence and obey us? Consider that we desire only your good and the good of the realm."

The princess had silenced her by saying, "As often as you command what is in accordance with faithfulness and truth, I will obey you, but if you order me to do what is contrary, then you are neither my parents nor my masters, and I will never obey you as such."

Since that day Margaret had asked to be excused from receiving any royal visitors, and went about her tasks in the Priory as usual. Those close to her may have remarked the added fervor with which she did them, even to the emptying of the swill, which she had to carry to the river, since there was no other means of sanitation on the island.

Finally the day came bringing for Bela and King Ottokar word from His Holiness, Pope Alexander IV: Margaret, Princess of the house of Arpad, was no longer under the obligation of fulfilling her vows, since it appeared that according to the word of her father, King Bela, she had pronounced them in the feeling that she was bound by promise. His Holiness sent his blessing to the princess, and his felicitations, should she now see fit to withdraw from the cloister to marry King Ottokar.

This was all Bela and Ottokar needed. They lost no time in sending for Father Marcellus, Prior General of the Dominican Order in Hungary and, as such, custodian of the spiritual welfare of all its members, even though Mother Catherine, the Prioress, presided on Hare's Island.

The day was gray and overcast when Father Marcellus was given the task of presenting the news to the princess and examining her to learn how exact her understanding of the matter was. The priest did not promise to use the persuasion with the princess that Ottokar had hoped for. The grave question of leaving a solitary life of sacrifice and prayer for one of marriage was a matter for the princess herself to decide.

"Allow me, Your Majesties," he said, "to remind you that the princess has never forgotten the merciful deliverance of this nation from the Tartars, and that she was then your hostage. She is fully aware of her calling. I dare say that she will not change her mind. Not if I know the princess."

It was later, that same gray day. A heavy fog over Hare's Island blurred the outlines of the little wooden dock. The Prior General drew his woolen cloak more closely about him against the damp chill that gnawed to the marrow. His spirit needed warming as much as his body, for certainly this errand was most distasteful to him. Moisture dripped from the bushes, and here and there a tree which had taken on an eerie shape loomed on the path to the Priory.

"It's a good day to be stirring about in this season of fast. Keeps the blood warm, my good man," Father Marcellus said, when he all but bumped into a farmer just as he was about to pull the Priory bell. Sister Portress answered his summons immediately, for he had tugged sharply on the rope.

"God's blessing and Our Lady's, Sister. It's bad business that brings me here to see Mother Prioress, Sister Helen, and her ladyship, Sister Margaret. A grave decision must be made by our princess. Better get down on your knees for us all, Sister," Father Marcellus said gravely. "And for King Bela as well."

There was nothing frightened about the princess when she answered the summons and seated herself in the Priory parlor between Mother Prioress and Sister Helen. In fact, she looked more at ease than the others, who held themselves rigid lest one detect their real thoughts in regard to the marriage of the princess.

After the customary greeting, the princess, for the last time making use of her high position, spoke first.

"Father Provincial, it is an errand of the court that has brought you here from my parents and King Ottokar. They have had word from His Holiness, and you have asked Mother Prioress and Sister Helen to witness my decision. Then I give it."

She drew a long breath and then continued steadily.

"You may take it for certainty, Father, regardless of the liberty His Holiness sees fit to grant, relying on my parents' word, that I prefer to die a thousand times rather than to obey the king in this matter. I have taken my first vows here because it is my firm belief God wishes me to be here. This is the life to which my parents consecrated me before my birth. No persuasion and no violence will be of any avail to make me renounce my calling."

Father Marcellus strove to hide the elation in his heart over the decision of the princess, but a smile lurked behind the turn of his words in spite of all their gravity.

"Sister Margaret, Princess of the house of Arpad," he said formally, "truly your ladyship speaks as a daughter worthy of your great ancestor, King Stephen, and our founder, Dominic. But, you know, your ladyship, all things you hold dear may fall from you by this decision."

"Yes, Father, I know."

"You have lost Stephen before this," went on the priest, "but he will come back again, I am sure. But the court will despise you, and make it appear that you have not the true welfare of your people at heart, and even here in the Priory, your way of life and your humility can be misunderstood. Yes, even the revenues of the Priory can be cut off, bringing dire poverty to all the Sisters."

Margaret faced him as firmly as ever.

"All those things can be made right, Father. But remember I am the King's hostage, the King of heaven and earth, at Whose beauty the sun and moon stand in wonder. Such is a privilege rarely accorded to a princess."

History records that some days later, lest ever again there be a question as to the validity of Margaret's vows, the chapel of the Priory blazed with color. Lace hung from the high altar, and candles glowed like jewels. Church prelates in magenta and red and simple curates in surplice and cassock had come to witness the solemn consecration of Margaret, Princess of the house of Arpad. The king and queen were absent, however, as were most of the court.

Jansci, his upturned nose giving him away even underneath a Dominican cowl and scapular, tugged at the sleeve of Father Paul as they knelt in the rear of the sanctuary.

"She's putting off the crown," he whispered, "that the Archbishop just blessed and set upon her head. Look, Father, she lies there where the fresh candles are at the foot of the Holy Rood. She's renounced everything ... *everything!* Forever!"

"No, boy," returned the elderly Dominican softly. *"She has accepted everything.'"*

As they made their way homeward to their lonely mission many miles east on the "alfold" or prairie land of the country, Father Paul looked upward. It was evening, with the sun sinking behind the hills of Buda. One white cloud lingered in the sky.

Father Paul mused aloud. "She has accepted everything. Some day it may be that the nation will come to see that she is lovelier than that white cloud, and the fairest where all are fair. Yes, boy, I even think I hear us proud Magyars gratefully saying in our hours of war and trial, 'Margaret, Margaret Arpad, pray for us!'"

THE END

CPSIA information can be obtained
at www.ICGtesting.com
Printed in the USA
LVHW081733100521
686999LV00032B/2548